# Are you hurtling towards God knows what?

by J.E.A. Wallace

# Are you hurtling towards God knows what?

by J.E.A. Wallace

Copyright©2018 J.E.A. Wallace
All Rights Reserved
Published by Unsolicited Press
First Edition Paperback.
Printed in the United States of America.

No part of this book may be reproduced or transmitted in any form or by any means without written permission from the publisher or author.

Cover Art by Benj Davies
Edited by S.R. Stewart

Attention schools and businesses: for discounted copies on large orders, please contact the publisher directly.

ISBN: 978-1-947021-67-9

For my family

# Poems

| | |
|---|---|
| The Light at the End of the Tunnel is a Different Taillight Every Time | 11 |
| Wearing Down the Corners of Sugar Lumps | 13 |
| Tsarina's Asylum | 15 |
| A Year's Worth of Postcards From London | 16 |
| Shoot | 20 |
| The longest serving temp at Data Entry Solutions keeps a synthesizer under their bed | 22 |
| Home is a forearm sweep across the forehead | 23 |
| Sea Song | 24 |
| The Escapologist's Daughter | 26 |
| The Ice Storm | 27 |
| Grace the Gratefully Yours | 29 |
| Murder at the Circus | 31 |
| Meanwhile, a few blocks from Times Square | 34 |
| A Buffalo is Your Co-Pilot | 36 |
| A Refrigerator Post-It Note in a Studio Apartment | 38 |
| The Battle of Vandam Street | 39 |
| Bryant Park Lovesong | 41 |
| Post-Apocalyptic Chandeliers | 43 |
| There is only ever one sport in the future | 45 |
| The Maiden Voyage of the U.S.S. Elpis-In-The-Jar | 46 |
| Based on a True Story | 48 |
| The 1.13 London to Necropolis Junction | 49 |
| Driving Mary Home | 51 |
| | |
| Acknowledgements | 53 |
| About the Author | 57 |
| About the Press | 58 |

# Are you hurtling towards God knows what?

by J.E.A. Wallace

# The Light at the End of the Tunnel is a Different Taillight Every Time

We are level with the horse drawn carriage
when the radio reports the weather
'There's rain coming down so hard ahead
it's stripping all the vultures of their feathers'

She mutters 'Hell' and shifts it up a gear
The black horse looks across and scowls
but we are only one of a hundred thousand
trying to win by fair or foul

To our left is a bishop on a motorbike
a cigarette between his teeth
He says something to the wild-eyed horse
something about the power of belief

But me and her we don't believe in nothing
only the horizon and the race
At the end said the radio is one row-boat
that takes you out to star strewn space

We don't know what happens to the left behind
I don't think we want to know
The raindrops crash on our windscreen
and a fierce wind starts to blow

'How far do you think 'til the finish line?
How long ago was it that we died
and woke up in this car doing eighty
with the sky tearing up outside?'

But all she says is 'hush, now'
Tightening her knuckles on the wheel
She promised me that we'd get there first
And my sister never welches on a deal

# Wearing Down the Corners of Sugar Lumps

Tell me a love story
Set in communist era Poland
Where little red cars trundle
Up and down grey state-built roads

She maybe works
In the Ministry of Information
And steals cafeteria sugar lumps
To feel their corners when she's waiting

At the clean efficient station
Where everything's on time
And the whistling Warsaw wind
Cleans the clocks of all in line

As she dreams of love stories
Set in communist era Poland
While little red cars trundle
Up and down grey state-built roads

He maybe lives
In the shoebox above hers
Building a piano nocturnally
With worn-down, worn-out fingers

Upon her return every night
There is one more note to hear
Of his song 'a communist love story'
That he wrote and made for her

Useless hearts dreaming of love stories
Set in communist era Poland
Like little red cars trundling
Up and down grey state-built roads

# Tsarina's Asylum

Towards the end of the speed-dating evening
She decides to tell him her name

'I am Anastasia Romanov.'

Drinks dance and tinkle
The fog of conversation bubbles
But no time at all passes in his face

'Who?'

His boredom tastes metallic
And sinks into her belly

'The great-great granddaughter of Nicholas the Tsar.'

The bell rings
And there is only her again

So with a lingering glance at the vodka behind the bar
And a sigh that would break the heart of a lion in Trafalgar

She rises
And drifts
Out into a London night
That has no patience with princesses

# A Year's Worth of Postcards From London

### *King's Cross, The 20<sup>th</sup> of March*

I do still get a little excited
When a train pulls out of the station
And we enter a beautiful limbo
Between departure and arrival

Where there's time to watch the colourful litter
Adorning the tangled embankments
Struggle just like all the rest
Of London to emerge

And shine beneath a springtime
Whose chilly cheerfulness
Is best observed from inside a train
Between departure and arrival

## *Greenwich, The 21ˢᵗ of June*

We could tie the sun to a stick
By the side of this empty road
Put our backs against the trees
To watch the green grass grow

And that dirty forgotten bottle
By the side of this empty road
I think is missing its ship
We should wait for it to show

Before we go anywhere...

### *Chiswick, The 22<sup>nd</sup> of September*

When summer's fallen asleep in the sky
And just lies there…

These giant albino mammoths
(Very slowly) crash the party
Dragging winter behind them
Like a sunburnt dehydrated cowboy

Underneath
Leaves run around on the pavement
Like cats at an old lady millionaire's house
And (finally)
The colours in this dirty old town look right

At night
The rain quietens the car alarms
And turns windows into percussion


Music to the ears
Of all the sunburnt dehydrated cowboys

*Balham, The 21$^{st}$ of December*

Outside
Icing sugar snow is falling
On a town that needs a little sweetening

The final touch
From the grey clouds' ancient fingers

The final touch?
This home of exhaust and invisible men?
I was under the impression there was further to go…

And then I realise

Throw a snowball in this town
And you'll hit your destiny

# Shoot

Her make-up holds off the rain as she stands there waiting to be murdered.

'Are we ready?'

Two bright yellow eyes, ten feet off the ground, stare at her as she shivers.

'Can we have some shelter?'

She watches strange shapes move in the blackness.

'Get a bleeding move on!'

Someone rushes out of the dark into the circle of light that surrounds her.

'Put this over your head.'

The patter on the paper reminds her of the day she left home for London for good.

'Lose the Guardian. Turn over. Speed.'

She can't help smiling in anticipation of the first words she'll ever say.

'Action!'

With arms outstretched, a monster stumbles towards her.

*'Is that you, Abeona?'*

```
The longest serving temp
 at Data Entry Solutions
   keeps a synthesizer
     under their bed
```

High heels and office shoes
Clatter on the overpass
Above centipede trains at Clapham Junction

We are shuffling pelicans in an empty reservoir

And if David Attenborough
Were to crouch by the wall to talk
In a hushed and soothing voice
Of our thoughtless, gut-fueled purpose

I would stop to ask, 'Could I do the soundtrack
for your programme?'

Because I would like
To spend my mornings
On the way to something good

# Home is a forearm sweep across the forehead

these
wannabe/ina/deckchair/midmornings
where you feel very far from home

from the slow crash of the waves
and the gentle swish of those dresses
on women who might open your eyes

and the crankle of ice cubes in glasses
that drip like a rainy windscreen
between your fingers

how did I become so far away from home?
wannabe/ina/deckchair/thismorning
please

# Sea Song

The New Zealand ladies
In their long silver dresses
Watch a ship catch fire from the shore

The orange flags it's flying now
Throw a hot 'hello' their way
(This is what their parasols are for)

Ragged rocks, pointed pebbles shift underneath their feet
They prefer the heat of summer, the orange of the beach
And they wonder why anyone
Would sail away to sea
In anything that catches fire

The lost English sailors
See long silver dresses
Floating like a promise on the shore

They point at their future
Wearing circular wings
(This is what their parasols are for)

Alabaster ash and fluttering flames swirl around their heads
They peek through it at their patient angels perched on the
    cliff's edge
And in every blackening eye
There's a flicker at the thought
Of their coming ascension into sky

# The Escapologist's Daughter

The escapologist's daughter
Slips quietly away
To hide in the
Giant alpenhorn
On the corner of the stage

As her father
Starts to writhe
And twist in
Water grim with bubbles

He emerges eventually
Still tied and dripping
With an apologetic 'ta-da!'

The escapologist's daughter
Sighs in the corner

And a beautiful note drifts away

## The Ice Storm

She looked pretty in her runaway party dress
It shone red beneath the dim chandeliers
And the blood beneath her fingernails chatters
Saying 'let's get out of here'

But her only hope is waiting at the bar
Fiddling with a scotch and looking bored
Grinding out another French-Canadian cigarette
Giving birth to a black hole in the floor

I am on the stage
Singing something about love
But the three of us we are beyond it
The ice storm outside is enough

Something of that freezing rain still lingers
When she takes a seat beside him
He is writing out their future on a napkin
Beneath the logo 'keep reaping grim'

She wraps her small white fingers
Around the cold jagged keys to his truck
He covers her hand with his and together they pray
For the late dramatic entrance of that old lush Lady Luck

I watch them leave from the stage
As I'm singing of the smooth and the rough
But the three of us we are beyond it
The ice storm outside is enough

# Grace the Gratefully Yours

(or 'How to Work a Roomful of Runaway Clowns')

The piano player's new and having trouble
Keeping the crowd in order
(A bunch of East German circus clowns
Waiting to cross the border)

Because it's about that time of night
When they wonder what they've done
They sob and honk their noses
And their heavy make-up runs

'For Christ's sake
Have another drink
The Stasi won't find you here
All of us
Will wait with you
'Til your escape balloon appears'

'Now may I introduce on stage –
"Grace the Gratefully Yours"
The woman with the voice borrowed
From another world's seashores.'

Into the squirting lapel flowers steps
A woman, and when she sings
She gently peels the sellotape
Off everybody's heartstrings

It's so quiet
Underneath her
Fear turns to a pin and drops
Shivering breath
Held in her hand
Until the shivering stops

When the last note fades she takes a bow and says:
'I believe your balloon's arrived,
You'd better hurry if you want to get across.
I'm so glad you survived.'

'Safe journey clowns, safe journey'

# Murder at the Circus

**Saturday**

Behind the big top, a dead man gathers snow
His memories leak into dirty, wet sugar
A cheer goes up from a close faraway
On break, between trees, a clown lights a cigar

Across air as sharp as Christmas-yet-to-come
A song starts to play and drift like black dragonflies
Though it might have been born a thousand years ago
Tonight it's only played to warm a cold band's eyes

The band's flickering fire is familiar
To the serious entertainers with the worn-out shoes
Who sail on, its lighthouse glow guiding them,
To drink and sleep and fair-do's

The unseen murdered's fingers are crooked but
There's no last message, no thought of retribution
Only as if a gentle tug on the ends of things
Is blood and breath's final execution

*Roll up!*

## Sunday

'Send in the clown'
Sighs the Ringmaster

Into the circling spotlight stumbles
A painted old man with glistening eyes
The smallest fish in the Marianas Trench

Outside, the meat wagon struggles
Across mudcastle tracks of now sleeping trucks
And the body in the back bounces gently on a bench

Even in there you could hear the laughter
That is whirling around the clown
Like a dream you'd have in a tornado

Offstage, Policemen wait patiently
Pinched faces ghouled between
Their tall black hats and their long black cloaks

'When all the hopes of your friends aren't enough to get
you what you want...'
Cries the Ringmaster

*Honk!*

## Monday

The only thing left
In the clown's cold tent
Is a mini-horse snuffling in the corner

Until 'The Greatest Trapeze' puts her head inside
And the only friends of the locked-up clown
Are reunited for the first time since

That night of swords & death & rain
When a face of ruined make-up
Held on to the skin of their teeth

The acrobat and the animal pick their courage off the floor
And somewhere an old man with a naked face hears
Approaching footsteps in his cavernous heart

*Encore!*

## Meanwhile, a few blocks from Times Square

The hotel room waits like a square in a maze
To capture the lost and with its walls
Beat desire for movement from you

The door creaks open like a chuckle
As another washed-up adventurer sighs
Seeing the box his exertions have earned him

The new guest is The Invisible Man
He throws his hat on the bed and
Starts unwinding his bandages

But there's a knock at the door
When he's only halfway through
Which brings a 're-do?' 'keep on?' panic

He decides it would be better to look nonchalant
And opens his suitcase and takes something out
Smiling at its sparkling in the swinging light

So that when the showgirl in peril bursts in
There's a bandaged man sitting on the window sill
Who's blowing an old, soft song on a golden saxophone

And even the room is impressed...
Could this be the adventurer's rest?

# A Buffalo is Your Co-Pilot

*Some days last forever - that's a legitimate measurement here*
*Even if you never take off - 'future astronaut' is still a career*

You and your best friend buffalo
At the top of the Empire State
It's the bridge of a ship making one last trip
Into space before it's too late
And you're the Captain of all you survey
On this blue Manhattan day

You and your best friend buffalo
Strolling through Central Park
Lost in a dream – but what does it mean
When you're riding on the back of a shark?
That with some modes of transport there's no fare to pay
On a gold Manhattan day

You and your best friend buffalo
On the steps of St. John the Divine
Inside, the poet is preparing to throw it
To the one they loved one last time
But on that subject you have nothing to say
On this purple Manhattan day

You and your best friend buffalo
Riding the subway home
Under the city that's sitting pretty
Where you and your old friend roamed
There is freedom from balance in the clattering sway
On a silver Manhattan day

*Some days last forever - that's a legitimate measurement here*
*Even if you crash land - 'former astronaut' is still a career*

# A Refrigerator Post-It Note in a Studio Apartment

Now Manhattan is my home, I need to buy my wife a dinghy. Because when the world comes to an end there's only one way off this island, and I don't want to be one of the puzzled, desperate crowd with fear inside my legs and eyes full of surprise. Trapped beneath tumbling shadows of crumbling towers, eaten alive by whatever's arrived to eat everybody alive. I want to be on the river sailing quietly upstate, holding my wife's trembling hand in my trembling hand, as faraway fires eat up the horizon and death black water laughs silently about us. Underneath a moon, that for all I know is the future, we drift towards another life; of raiding stores and stealing cars and driving to Vancouver. But tonight I hear my wife put on the kettle in the kitchen, while outside our window all of history is turning. Now Manhattan is my home, I need to buy my wife a dinghy.

# The Battle of Vandam Street

On Vandam Street in the pouring rain
They watched his window with eyes of flame

Inside
Time was getting was short
Cigarettes were being smoked to extinction

He violently wished not to have to go
To the merry gentlemen in the street below

Deep inside
He knew nobody
Chooses the hour of their damnation

He looked at his dog asleep on the bed
And softly scratched its dreaming head

Deep inside
It was shouting down
The moon in a war of attrition

But it stirred as he quietly dragged
His shadow down the stairs that sagged

Inside
His dog put its face to the window
And bared teeth that shone like salvation

The tumbling glass flickered eyes of flame
On Vandam Street in the pouring rain

# Bryant Park Lovesong

At the top of an empty skyscraper
A man tunes an electric guitar

He's one silhouette among many
Although the tiny movements
Of his twisting, tuning fingers
Make him the only possible monster

The last light left in the city
On top of a faraway crumbling tower
Swings around and illuminates
The crouching man
Wincing with listening
Surrounded by beaten up instruments

By the time the glow from the lighthouse has vanished
The electric guitar is in tune
The man reaches up
To push a button that clunks
On an enormous obsolete monitor
(everything's obsolete in this room)
A flickering straight green line appears
Beneath the numbers two, zero, zero and zero

He knows the girl he still loves
Is sitting in that year by her radio
(he remembers how lonely she was that night)
And he knows this is his last chance to tell
Of this impossible-to-contain that he feels for her
He must get her heart beating again
He looks around
At the instruments about him
And wonders how his song
Will begin

# Post-Apocalyptic Chandeliers

The chandeliers constantly jingle
Inside this house in abandoned New York
Shaken by starlings that tear past
The cracked window teeth of the mansion's maw

There is life in here as well
It comes from the dreams of the ghost
Now descending the collapsing stairs
A polar opposite of clumsy shadow

The crooked corridor paintings
Watch as it drifts by
Its determination casts
No reflection in their eyes

Once again it makes its way
Into the sunlit ballroom
Whose broken glass is everywhere
Like a smashed up crystal tomb

The skeleton of the piano
Is wearing a menacing smile
As if to say 'Oh, you again?
Are we giving it one more try?'

But a ghost knows how to ignore things
And focus on the task at hand
It gathers all the life in its dreams
To speak the name of a woman

Who hasn't been seen since long before
These parts were blown apart
Who had promised to return
If only he would ask

# There is only ever one sport in the future

I'm putting my fighting money on the smaller robot; the half-finished girl in the oil stained coat. I know the monstrous metal thing stood opposite her was built to fight wars (was built to end wars in the time it takes to say, 'what the hell is that?') and I see the inexplicable drool falling from its teeth is burning little holes in the floor. I know the thing riveted to its right arm, a grotesque gun pulsing with smoke and possibilities, is twice as big as the girl. And I see all she has is a wonky but sweet sort of smile and eyes so wide and blue you'd think there was a planet somewhere missing two lagoons. But I know how these things go. I'm putting my fighting money on the smaller robot.

```
   The Maiden Voyage of the
   U.S.S. Elpis-In-The-Jar
```

She was sick
and very tired
when she volunteered for 'Save Us!'

When she woke
They had replaced
her insides with titanium

Where they told her
'You are ready
to work down the black hole mine

I'm afraid
it's our last hope
you are the only one who lived'

Now she's alone
apart from robots
on a beyond belief sized spaceship

wondering
for the first time
if she can trust her gut

So she whispers
to the robots
who are petrified with learning

as they stand
in silent awe
of the approaching black that swirls

'It's what you fear
you know of the unknown
that's scrambling your circuits

Let's know nothing
but hope together
and mine our future from the dark'

# Based on a True Story

I fled my daughter's cremation with her skull
I am something of a hoarder &
Although I'd felt nothing before beneath
Sky blue as a pool in a soap opera

Inside a building where wrists hang in fingers
& it's dark like a TV in the sun
When flames began to lick her bones
I had to take her face & run

I put my hands into the fire
It tore the cuffs from my shirt
I took the thing where my daughter's dreams lived
I don't remember if it hurt

I ran past widening eyes & opening mouths
I said 'Sorry' in between
The laughing that was coming like breathing
The echoes where my feet had been

Now I am running down the middle of the road
& the ivory in my hands is shining
When I look into the spaces where her eyes were
I swear I see them smiling

# The 1.13 London to Necropolis Junction

It wasn't until it was vanishing
Between the ancient trees
That I realised
I had left myself
Sleeping on the train

So here I am

Standing
Empty handed
On an
Empty platform

I could be wrong
But I think the man
I'm meeting's crouching
Underneath that willow tree

The shadows of branches are scars on his face
His eyes
        Discarded bottle tops
                      From some forgotten picnic

      Everything's so still      Everything's moving
    Perpetual dust skipping     Through trembling air
       Playing catch-up to a long gone parade

The gravel burns
Gently with a shimmer
These are the remains of clouds
                            Fallen
              Like the angels
A long time ago

He tilts his head
I smile and shrug
And make a letter W
As used by castaways
On the wrong end of a telescope

Aye,
It's a beautiful day to be unprepared

For an end
Or for a beginning

# Driving Mary Home

Driving Mary home
From *Who Wants To Be A Millionaire?*
She lost out on fifty grand
And she says she doesn't care

But in her eyes are faster cars
In faraway adventures
Burying alarm clocks
And too much pain to mention

Where she ends and
The window begins
Is being blurred by
A rainy neon wind

I'd crossed my fingers waiting
Back in the polar car park
Willing out a star from the satellites
As it was getting dark

She stirs and rests her head on me
To hear my breathing in
Under service station castles
She begins to softly sing

*When this journey ends*
*In a sinking pillow sigh*
*My eyes will close themselves*
*As this storm rolls grumbling by*

Our hearts beat along
To the windscreen wiper night
I try to make mine spell out
*We will be alright*

# Acknowledgements

'The Light at the End of the Tunnel is a Different Taillight Every Time' first published in *Illumen*

'Wearing Down the Corners of Sugarlumps' first published in *Illumen*

'Tsarina's Asylum' first published in *Four Cornered Universe*

'A Year's Worth Of Postcards From London' first published in *Lowestoft Chronicle*

'Shoot' first published in *Southpaw Journal*

'The longest serving temp…' first published in *The Write Place At The Write Time*

'Home is a Forearm Sweep Across The Forehead' first published in *Irk*

'Sea Song' first published in *blankpages*

'The Escapologist's Daughter' first published in *Stanley The Whale*

'The Ice Storm' first published in *Irk*

'Grace The Gratefully Yours' first published in *The Minetta Review*

'Murder At The Circus' first published in *Hidden Chapters*

'Meanwhile, a few blocks from Times Square...' first published in *Lowestoft Chronicle*

'A Buffalo Is Your Co-pilot' first published in *The Minetta Review*

'A Refridgerator Post-it Note...' first published in *Midnight Screaming*

'The Battle of Vandam Street' first published in *The Write Place At The Write Time*

'Bryant Park Lovesong' first published in *The Write Place At The Write Time*

'Post-Apocalyptic Chandeliers' first published in *The Write Place At The Write Time*

'There is only ever one sport in the future' first published in *Brand Literary Journal*

'The Maiden Voyage of the U.S.S. Elpis-In-The-Jar' first published in *Illumen*

'Based on a True Story' first published in *Dark Rivers*

'The 1.13 London to Necropolis Junction' first published in *Horn & Ivory*

'Driving Mary Home' first published in *The Write Place At The Write Time*

## About the Author

J.E.A. Wallace has been a hotel night porter, an abattoir security guard, and a barman in the House of Lords. Born and raised in England, he is now a happily married poet who lives and writes in New York City.

## About the Press

Unsolicited Press was founded in 2012 and is based in Portland, Oregon. The press seeks to produce outstanding poetry, fiction, and creative nonfiction. Learn more at www.unsolicitedpress.com.